MAVIS SNELSON

HABIT FORMATION

The Essential Guide on How to Develop Success Habits, Discover How You Can Break Free From Bad Habits and Achieve Your Full Potential

Descrierea CIP a Bibliotecii Naţionale a României
MAVIS SNELSON
    HABIT FORMATION. The Essential Guide on How to
Develop Success Habits, Discover How You Can Break Free
From Bad Habits and Achieve Your Full Potential / Mavis
Snelson – Bucharest: Editura My Ebook, 2021
    ISBN

MAVIS SNELSON

HABIT FORMATION

The Essential Guide on How to Develop Success Habits, Discover How You Can Break Free From Bad Habits and Achieve Your Full Potential

My Ebook Publishing House
Bucharest, 2021

TABLE OF CONTENTS

INTRODUCTION

When you really think about it, most of life is something we do out of habit. From the moment we wake up in the morning to the actions we take throughout the day – our "morning routine", or "regular breakfast", our "typical commute", the "daily grind" at work – the habits we develop literally control about 95% our actions. These types of unconscious thoughts determine what we think, how we feel and how we behave in nearly every situation we find ourselves in.

Because our habits dictate all the small details that make up our everyday lives, they also are directly related to the bigger issues in our lives, such as how much money we earn, the kind of person we marry or live with, our physical condition and health, and every other area of our lives.

Our habits determine our character, the type of person we project to the rest of the world and, ultimately, our destiny. So if we embrace bad habits – those habits which have a negative impact on who we are – then those same habits will prevent us from achieving excellence in our lives, holding us back from reaching our fullest potential.

It's only by breaking bad habits and replacing them with good habits that we can ultimately succeed in life and be the people we were truly meant to be. The purpose of this guide is to show you how to break bad habits – any sort of bad habit, from those that are damaging to your health, like smoking or not wearing a seatbelt, to those that affect your self-esteem, such as negative thinking or overeating – and replace them with positive behaviors that can become part of your daily life and finally cause you to see the results you truly want.

Albert Einstein once said that the definition of insanity was performing the same task over and over again and expecting a different result. When you keep repeating the same bad habits, you would have to be crazy to think that anything will ever change for you. "Breaking the Habit" will show you how to end the madness and start living your life to its fullest by abandoning bad habits and replacing them with positive ones.

Wanting to Break the Habit

I want to begin with a personal story. When I was a younger person, I was a heavy smoker. I began smoking in college – it was during the 1980s and smoking didn't have the cultural stigma it does now – and continued well into my 30s. I knew that smoking was bad for my health. Indeed, I would wake up in the morning with a hacking cough, would feel breathless throughout the day, and by the time I got home at night I was exhausted, even if I hadn't particularly exerted myself during the day.

Then there was the chemical dependency I developed to the nicotine contained in cigarettes. If I went without a cigarette for longer than an hour or so, I would become jittery, irritable and would even begin to get panicked. It was only when I gave my body the drug it needed (yes, nicotine is a drug and actually is more addictive than heroin) that I was able to return to my "normal" self.

During the 15 years that I smoked, I quit smoking literally hundreds of times. I became something of an expert at quitting smoking, even if I always backslid into the same dirty and unhealthy habit sooner or later. Cold turkey, hypnotism, acupuncture, the patch, nicotine-laced chewing gum, you name it, I tried it.

Every time I tried to quit smoking, I truly believed that this was it, I was going to stop and put this terrible habit behind me once and for all. But it never stuck. Ultimately my desire to smoke became stronger than my desire to stop.

Until one day I came to a stunning discovery. I realized that I truly didn't *want* to smoke anymore. It was simply something that didn't fit into my life, either then or in the future that I saw for myself. Right then and there, I made a commitment to stop smoking (It was easier than ever before because I truly had no desire to smoke anymore) and, after a few days of uncomfortable withdrawal symptoms, I was finished with it.

That was more than 10 years ago and I haven't had a single cigarette since. Even the smell of somebody else smoking is enough to send me scurrying away. When I see others smoking – while I try not to judge -- I often can't help but wonder why they can't see themselves the way others perceive them. If they could, perhaps they, too, could reach the point where ending their bad, destructive habit was not only possible, but easy.

"Bad" Habits vs. "Good" Habits

So how does one define a "bad" habit, and what qualities separate those from "good" habits? In most cases, the distinction is obvious. A habit is a "bad" habit if:

- It is destructive, harmful or poses a short or long-term danger to you or somebody else.

- It negatively impacts your self-esteem, the way others view you, and your overall reputation as a good or bad person.

- Is a pattern of undesirable behavior acquired through frequent repetition.

Usually, bad habits begin innocently. I smoked my first cigarette because my college roommate smoked and I was curious about what it tasted and felt like. But bad habits have a tendency to quickly snowball.

A single bad habit can act as a magnet to others. People who smoke often tend to drink. People who drink sometimes use profanity or are rude to other people. People who are rude and profanity might hang out at casinos or horseracing tracks.

People who gamble may be more likely to frequent prostitutes or take drugs. Soon, something that started out as a quirk or a one-off has escalated into a lifestyle that is self-destructive, damages your reputation and ultimately can ruin your career, your family life, your health and even end your life.

Examples of Bad Habits

Practically any habit that can be considered "good" can have a "bad" counterpart:

- Destructive personal habits like smoking, drinking and abusing drugs

- Overeating or not living a healthy lifestyle

- Making poor financial decisions

- Gambling

- Procrastinating

- Being addicted to sex or pornography

- Failing to live in a positive manner/Taking a negative view of your world

In short, anything that interferes with your ability to live a happy and healthy life can be considered a bad habit.

When Is a Habit Really An Addiction?

People who are addicted to drugs, alcohol, sex, gambling or other self- destructive behavior frequently point to the physical and psychological addiction that prevents them from overcoming their bad habits.

But you don't need to have a chemical or psychological dependency to have an addiction. Addiction is defined as "The state of being enslaved to a habit or practice ....to such an extent that its cessation causes severe trauma."

So, in fact, any bad habit is an addiction because it enslaves us, preventing us from achieving our highest potential. Make no mistake: There will be consequences for reversing any bad habit. Yet these are nothing to fear.

Pain is temporary; quitting lasts forever.

Our Need for Habitual Behavior, Habits and Beliefs

Habits are not only useful, but we actually rely on our routines to function in our daily lives. Physiologists tell us that of the 11,000 signals we receive from our senses, our brain only consciously processes about 40. So our brains use the rote familiarity of habits so that we can focus on other "higher value" activities.

Things like walking, chewing our food, and talking don't require the kind of mental focus that solving math problems or playing video games do. These activities we take for granted are actually habits we have developed that are performed without conscious intent.

Social habits work the same way. Most people will take a shower at the same time every day or always drive the same route to work. These habits are performed essentially without conscious thought. Negative habits – like overeating, smoking or driving too fast – work the same way. We rarely think about these things, even when they are putting us in danger or damaging our health or well-being.

Using Habits to Achieve Success

Oftentimes, we are not able to even perceive that we have bad habits. Have you ever known or worked with somebody who has poor personal hygiene or had a friend who drank or partied too much? Usually, those people don't consciously decide to perform their bad habit. They just do it out of ... well, habit!

When we take the time to recognize our own bad habits, take corrective action and replace them with good, positive and healthy habits, the result is permanent change that pays dividends to our health, prosperity and happiness for the rest of our lives.

Imagine being a fit and active person who works out daily without even thinking about it. Or someone who always makes the right food choices, doesn't get into financial trouble, studies thoroughly for every exam, performs their work duties without flaw automatically, and so on. Isn't that something that is desirable? If you could make healthy, positive choices all the time without even thinking about it, your life would be much, much easier, wouldn't it?

Once you can replace your bad habits with good habits, you can also eliminate the stress and anxiety that those bad habits cause in your life so that you can finally achieve the feelings of happiness and well-being that you have always desired.

You deserve to be happy. In your heart, you know that to be true. Breaking your bad habits and replacing them with good ones can help you achieve that happiness.

Are you ready to get started?

"IT TAKES 21 DAYS TO CHANGE A HABIT"

You are about to take a journey that is literally going to transform the way you live. Once you embrace the process of converting your bad habit or habits into good ones, the rewards you reap will be enormous and lifelong.

It doesn't matter how long you have had your bad habits. They could be something you have done since childhood, such as lying or biting your fingernails. As long as you can recognize that the habit is destructive and genuinely want to convert it into something positive, you can change any bad habit into a good habit.

Changing Habits

Everybody has bad habits. It doesn't matter if it's the Pope or George Clooney, the Dalai Lama or the Archbishop of

Canterbury, people are human, they occasionally make mistakes, and these mistakes can often develop into bad habits.

The problem isn't that you have bad habits. That's normal. What's causing you unhappiness and psychic pain is that up to this point you have been unwilling to make a genuine commitment to change.

You truly can do anything you put your mind to. The human will is indomitable and the changes that lie ahead are going to surprise and amaze you. All it takes is the will to do it.

What's So Special about 21 Days?

You may have heard that it takes 21 days to change a habit. That's one reason residential rehab centers for drug and alcohol abuse usually last 21 days. It takes that long for the body to flush out the toxic substances that it is addicted to. But it's also how long it takes for the mind to expel the toxic negative thoughts that cause it to cling to bad habits so that they can replace them with positive ones.

Three weeks or a month also is a good timeframe to work with when changing habits because it corresponds with our calendar system. If you target the first day of the month for the beginning of a habit change, then it's a simple matter to use that month as a framework to work on your objective ("I'm going to get this done by Week 2, that done by Week 2 ..." and so on).

Not every bad habit requires 21 days or a month to change. Some can take longer and some can take less time. For example, if your goal is to get out of bed a half hour earlier each day so you can make your mornings more productive, you probably can make this a habit within a week to 10 days.

But habits that go deeper into your character – such as being kinder to your spouse, or becoming a more spiritually centered person, or losing the extra weight that is making you obese and out of shape and replacing it with muscle – can take months or even years to achieve fully.

Creating a Fresh Start

Everybody has experienced the frustration and feelings of helplessness that come with having bad habits. When you are doing something you know is bad for you, but you do it anyway, it can cause a psychic hurt that can affect your self-esteem ("I must be a bad person because I always (Insert Bad Habit Here").

But at the same time, bad habits can *always* be overcome, as long as you are persistent and apply the right strategies, which will be outlined in detail in this guide.

When Habits are Controlling and Ruining Your Life

Every bad habit can be damaging to your physical and/or mental health, but some are more serious than others. While biting your fingernails may not be sanitary or particularly healthy, it probably isn't going to kill you the way shooting heroin or eating fast food every day eventually will.

Making bad choices almost always leads to making more bad choices. Even the most innocuous poor decision can sometimes lead to a downward spiral that leaves you wondering what just happened. Even the smallest of bad habits can have a profound negative effect on the rest of your life.

Cheating on your taxes, for example, can lead to "rounding up" on your hourly timesheet, which can lead to "borrowing" from your company's petty cash fund, which can lead to changing the books so that additional funds are diverted into your private accounts. You've graduated from a tax cheat into an embezzler!

The Will to Choose

You always have a choice, however. Even the most degenerate, emaciated, drug-addled street junkie or someone

400 lbs overweight with diabetes, high blood pressure and congestive heart failure can make the decision to turn their life around. That's one of the gifts of being a rational, thinking human.

Thanks to our ability to reason, only humans have the ability to end bad habits and convert them into good ones. And it's never, ever too late. All it requires is the will to choose and being brave enough to make positive changes in your life. That's the hard part. As you will soon see, the rest is easy.

Goal Setting

Once you cross the Rubicon and decide to affect positive change in your life, all you need to do is to follow the process laid out in this guide and you can achieve your goals within whatever timeline you choose.

Goal setting is when you apply realistic expectations to your desired outcome. In Chapter 5, entitled "The Game Plan", you are going to learn how to develop practical, concrete goals that you can follow every step of the way that ultimately lead to good habits and a better, happier and healthier life.

Accepting Responsibility

None of this happens in a vacuum, however. Any bad habits you have are yours and yours alone. Blaming other people or situations for your bad habits will do nothing to help you overcome them.

Maybe your mother and father weren't responsible parents. Maybe your husband or wife is indifferent to you sexually. Maybe you were bullied in school. So what?

While these things may have contributed to your bad habits, they aren't going to help you overcome them. In fact, any unwillingness to accept responsibility for your bad habits will ultimately sabotage your efforts and prevent you from achieving your goal. Honesty and maturity are two key factors that separate those people who can successfully change their lives and those who are destined to continually repeat the same mistakes over and over again.

Searching for Answers

In the same way that you alone are responsible for your own bad habits, in nearly every instance you alone lack the power to overcome your bad habits entirely by yourself. In some way, shape or form, eventually you are going to require the help of other people.

When we are struggling with personal problems that are consequences of our bad habits, there's a tendency to circle the wagons and try to take care of things on your own. This is truly a bad idea.

It's perhaps ironic that you are responsible for your own bad habits but you need the help of others – whether it's in the form of health care, nursing, coaching, support or just information from books or websites – in order to make things better. But seeking out and getting the answers and help that you need is an essential step in your healing process.

Over the course of the next 21 days, there are going to be a lot of changes that you are going to experience. Not all of them are going to fall within your "comfort zone". You may be accustomed to being completely self- sufficient and prefer to work on fixing your own problems entirely independently of anybody else.

In the words of Dr. Phil, "How's that working out for you?"

NEGATIVE EMOTIONS AND POSITIVE FEELINGS

Many people aren't even aware that they have bad habits. They just wonder why the universe keeps conspiring against them and causing them to have such terrible luck. They never even realize that in most cases they are the cause of all of their own problems through the bad habits they keep repeating.

In order to make genuine, positive improvements in your life, the first step is to develop self-awareness. You can't effectively choose new habits if you aren't even aware of what your current habits are. In this section, we are going to walk through the process of becoming more aware of your thoughts, feelings and actions so that you can see the connection between them and the things that are happening to you in your life.

By developing this sense of self-awareness, you can move your subconscious thoughts and feelings into the conscious sphere of your thinking, analyze these thoughts so that they can make the connection between your bad habits and their consequences to your life, and then choose new behaviors based on what you discover about yourself.

What Is It You Want?

Everybody wants something out of life. For some, it may be a happy, fulfilling marriage. For others, it's unlimited wealth and power. For still others, it could be spiritual enlightenment or a feeling of closeness to a higher power.

As the Rolling Stones once sang, "You can't always get what you want/But if you try sometime/You just might find/You get what you need."

What is it you want more than anything else out of life? Try to think in "big picture" terms. Rather than simply wanting to stop smoking, your goal may be to achieve optimal health. Rather than just to pay off a staggering amount of debt, think of your goal as enjoying financial security or even prosperity for the rest of your life.

Creating Self Awareness

Once you have identified some overriding objectives – think global, not local – the next step is to understand what has been preventing you from achieving these goals. This can be achieved through a number of methods, including:

- **Reflection** – Think about past experiences and then use your understanding of how you behaved during those events so that you can apply what you learned from them to future situations.

- **Friends and Family** – Open lines of communication with others by asking people you trust if they also see your bad habit.

- **Compare Yourself With Others** – Think about people who already have the good habits you want and consider what they do differently than you when confronted to relevant situations.

- **Available Information** – Are there any books, courses or videos that can help you achieve your objective? What sort of things do you find when you search online?

- **Personal Beliefs** – If you are a spiritual person or have religious beliefs, call upon these to help you along your journey toward self- discovery. Even people who are non-religious can benefit from surrendering themselves to the will of the universe, or a "higher power" if you prefer to call it that.

- **Start a Journal** – It's nearly impossible to remember each thought and breakthrough you have along the way. Keep a journal so you can keep track of your progress and refer back to what you have learned.

- **Create Measurable Objectives** – Start to think about what success will look like. What measurable event has to occur for you to believe you have successfully achieved your objective?

There may be more than one bad habit that you want to change. If so, you may want to prioritize and attack these one at a time. Trying to fix too many things at once can dilute your efforts so that little or nothing substantive is accomplished. Once you learn how to overcome your first bad habit, however, the later ones will be easier to break.

Keeping a Habit Diary

Once you have selected a single bad habit that you want to break, the next step is to develop an awareness about the habit as it applies to you. One way to do this is to keep a Habit Diary, which is simply a record of how you performed against your objective.

For example, if your goal is to stop smoking, you will want to start to keep track of how many cigarettes you smoked per day and what time you smoked them. If you want to stop overeating, write down everything that you eat throughout the day. If your goal is to stop telling lies, every time you lie to somebody, write down what you said, who you said it to and, if known, why you said it.

This type of tangible information will help you understand where you stand in terms of your bad habit. In many cases, the results you find and the patterns you notice may be shocking.

Root Causes of Bad Habits

After you have identified a bad habit and begun to track it in your daily life, this will often lead to a search for the root causes of your bad habit. While you don't want to blame other people or situational environments for your bad habits – you own them, they are entirely yours alone – you can still try to understand what is triggering these bad habits.

For example, if your bad habit is that you use rough language too often, pay attention to when you find yourself swearing. Who are you with? Who do you never swear in front of? Or if your bad habit is that you are a compulsive gambler, what are the triggers that get you thinking about gambling? Do you have to pass by a casino or racetrack on your way home from work every day? Is there a particular convenience store where you always buy your lottery tickets?

Understanding the situations and triggers that cause us to act on our bad habits will be useful later when we are working to end them.

Consequences

The next step of developing self-awareness about your bad habit is something I like to call "Putting two and two together".

Earlier, you thought about what it was you wanted out of life. You identified some global objectives that you wanted to work toward. Perhaps you were able to envision an idealized life for yourself or there is somebody you admire who is living the type of life you want for yourself.

Now I want you to think about what is it that is preventing you from achieving this ideal. What is it about your bad habit that is standing in the way of you and your objective? In other words, I want you to "do the math" so that you can see exactly how your actions are directly causing the consequence that you are experiencing.

It is simply cause and effect. Your bad habits are the cause. The effect is that you aren't living the life you want. Yet for your entire life up to this point, you haven't been able to put two and two together and come to the realization that your actions are causing your consequences.

Until now!

Making a Commitment to Yourself

So far, so good.

You've identified something about yourself that you want to change, you've engaged in the process of self-awareness and it has led to the understanding that the actions that you personally are taking are the cause of the consequences you are experiencing.

30

What's left is for you to make a personal and durable commitment to changing those actions so that you can change those consequences. I'm not talking about simply saying some magic words or making another empty promise. What's required is for you to make a solemn and irreversible commitment – a contract with yourself, if you prefer – that obligates you to achieving your objective.

It's not necessary that you have to commit to changing on the spot, here and now, and that you will never perform that bad habit ever again. That's not going to work because your life is too complicated for that. It probably has taken you years, if not a lifetime, to get to where you are today. Simply promising to yourself that you are going to change right now is about as effective as spitting into the wind.

Instead, take some time to think about what you are promising. Ponder on why it's important that you succeed. How will your life be different when you have broken your bad habit? What will be the consequences if you continue to engage in the bad behavior?

Excuses and Inner Dialogue

Once you have made up your mind and are committed to making positive changes in your life (which won't take place right away or all at once ... This is a process), the next step is to stop making excuses or allowing negative inner dialogue to influence your decision making.

You already have come to grips with the fact that you are solely responsible for your behavior. It's not your environment, how you were raised, or how other people have treated you. These are the types of excuses and negativity that people use as a crutch in order to justify their bad habits. When you have made a genuine commitment to yourself to change, they no longer have any power over you.

Start paying attention to what you tell yourself right before and during the bad habit you want to break. What excuses do you automatically bring up? What kind of rationality do you use that allows you to do whatever it is you want to stop doing? These are the thoughts and feelings you will need to overcome.

HOW GOOD HABITS WILL IMPACT YOUR LIFE

Congratulations! The hardest part is over. Increasing your self-awareness to the point where you realize that you have to make a change is the hardest part of the self-improvement process. Unlike 99.99% of people with bad habits, you are now able to admit you have a problem and accept full responsibility for dealing with it.

The last chapter was the most difficult part of the change process. It's natural for people not to want to admit weakness or to deny they have a problem that needs to be addressed. Yet making this breakthrough is an essential part of the recovery process. And you have made it!

In this section, we are now going to turn our attention to creating an environment of positivity that is going to give you the strength and support you need to nurture yourself to a new, health and life-affirming habit.

The Benefit of Good Habits

You may recall that about 95% of the things we do every day are out of habit. When you can eliminate bad habits and replace them with good ones, positive things will start to happen to you automatically.

Legendary motivational speaker Earl Nightingale once said that if you are willing to devote just one hour per day to studying within your field, you can get to a leadership position within your chosen profession in just three years. One hour per day of study will make you a national authority in five years. And within seven years, you can be one of the most recognized experts in the world.

Reading an hour per day in your field translates to about one book per week. So you can see that something as simple as developing a positive habit like reading an hour per day can not only bring positivity, but can actually transform your life.

Like a commercial airliner that has all of the significant flight information programmed into its onboard computer so that it can fly on automatic pilot, the good habits we develop are the "mental software" that will allow us to reach our ultimate objectives without even having to think about it.

Step 1: Discovering Your Purpose

Developing self-awareness allowed you to become more familiar with your current bad habits and connect them with the consequences that are holding you back from achieving your ultimate objectives.

The next step is to create goals for yourself that will help you move away from bad habits and move toward the kind of life you truly want for yourself. Goal setting is most effective if you first have a positive vision and purpose for your life. This will allow you to stay inspired to work on "smaller" goals and habits that build up to your overall objective. This process can be expressed with this diagram:

Purpose ➡ *Vision* ➡ *Goals* ➡ *Habits*

The beginning point is to discover your purpose. To do so, ask yourself these questions:

- Who am I?
- Why am I here?
- What do I want to accomplish with my life?

- What would make me feel most fulfilled?

- What do I value more than anything?

- Do I believe in God, a higher power, or the will of the universe?

- How does this affect the choices I make?

Step 2: Creating Your Vision Statement

Think about the answers you came up with. Write them down somewhere and try to organize them so that there is some sort of order or pattern. This is how you define your *belief system*, which is the overriding purpose behind your life.

If you can't see the pattern right away, try reflecting on these additional questions:

- How would I choose to live if I could do anything in the world?

- If you never had to worry about money again, how would you spend your days and night?

- At the end of your life, what will you point to as your most important accomplishment?

- What would you like people to say about you at your funeral?

Are you starting to see it now? What you are discovering is your vision of how you want your life to be. The next step is to arrange that vision into a single sentence or paragraph – called a *Vision Statement* -- that defines what you want out of life.

Here are a few examples of vision statements that others have come up with from the website Tita Eda (https://sites.google.com/site/titaeda/sample-vision-statements):

"I am a housewife and also working, I want to balance my family and professional life - both. I want to become a successful human being. I want to improve my personality, and also the growth of the company and myself. I want to earn money to make my family and society happy."

"My personal vision is to use myself as an example to impact positive attitudes and share my can do and never die attitude with whoever comes crosses my path in life. I wish that I can inspire and motivate them to discover and develop their potential and live life to fullness. In order for this vision to be fulfilled, I need to get a career first so that I can help more by helping thyself first."

"I myself want to be a true leader and help all the people who come to me. I want to complete my PHD program in human resources. I want to be a motivational leader and provide training programs to the corporate world. I love to be a truthful, family loving person and want to visit across the world and enjoy life."

What does your Vision Statement look like?

Step 3: Building Your Power Goals

Your Vision Statement is where you want to go. Your *Power Goals* are how you plan to get there.

To develop these Power Goals, let's return for a moment to the bad habit that you identified that you want to break. Think about how this bad habit affects you in each of these areas of your life:

Health Relationships Money/Finances
Work/Career Personal Development
Friends/Social Life Family Life Spiritual

Not every bad habit will have an impact on every aspect of your life, but you may be surprised on how deeply damaging your bad habits can be.

To develop your Power Goals, simply complete the connection between how breaking your bad habit will cause an improvement in each particular area that you have identified.

For example, let's assume the bad habit you want to break is that you are addicted to gambling:

Health: Your addiction to gambling causes you to lose sight of what's important in life, become anti-social, become financial unstable and most likely end up in debt.

Power Goal: When you break the bad habit of gambling, you will become more positive in life, create positive goals and stop wasting money (in the end the house always wins).

Relationships: Gambling takes a toll on your relationships and financial situation.

Power Goal: Once you are done with gambling, you will work to reconnect with your friends, family, partner and improve your financial situation.

Continue with this exercise with each category right down the line. If there is no direct correlation between your bad habit and a particular area of your life, just skip it and go to the next one.

Why Goals are Essential for Happiness

When you compile a list of Power Goals, they will provide the structure upon which you will build your Game Plan for achieving your vision statement. Once this journey has been broken down into smaller, achievable steps, you will be able to not only break your bad habit, but essentially live your life on autopilot.

As long as you follow your plan consistently and habitually, your long-term success is virtually assured. Of course, things can still go wrong and life will continue to throw the occasional curve ball at you. But because you have been able to break a bad habit and replace it with a good one -- and repeat the process over and over again until all of your bad habits are in your past – you will have the strength and personal determination to overcome any setback.

Researching Your Path

When it comes to achieving your Power Goals, knowledge is power. The more information you have about your objective, and about how other people have achieved it, the more tools you will have at your disposal when it comes time to act on your goals.

Spend time on the Internet researching everything you can about your goals. Look especially for blogs and forums that are related to your key bad habit. Given the size and scope of the web, there will absolutely be many sites that are specifically devoted to any particular problem. You are sure to find a wealth of information and inspiring personal stories that will help motivate you.

STOP PROCRASTINATING AND GET MORE DONE

If the hardest part about changing a bad habit into a good one is admitting that you have a problem, then the second hardest part is staying focused on your objectives. Life has a tendency to get in the way of our intentions and it's easy to become distracted or fall back into our bad behavior.

It's also very easy to *say* that you want to affect positive change in the abstract, but continually put off acting on that goal. This type of procrastination can add months or even years to your achieving your objective. It may even derail your habit-breaking process altogether.

The Consequences of Procrastination

Procrastination is just one more excuse that people use to avoid doing the hard work of achieving their objectives. In the same way that nobody else is responsible for your bad habits –

you own them and it's up to you to resolve them – putting off the inevitable is just another way of shirking responsibility.

When you procrastinate ("I'll start next week" or "I'm not ready yet"), you are only cheating yourself. You may have all the motivation in the world to change your life, but without direct and immediate action, you will never achieve your overall objectives.

Power Goals

Often, procrastination is a problem because people think about the big issues rather than break them down into smaller, more doable steps. It's like the old saying goes: How do you eat an elephant? One bite at a time!

When you think, "Oh, my goodness, I have to stop drinking" or "I can't believe I have so much debt to pay off" or whatever your bad habit, it can be daunting. But by breaking your goals into a series of easier steps and arranging them into a timed sequence of events, you can affect positive change without having to slay all of your demons at once.

Motivation and Enthusiasm

It's helpful to have motivation to keep you on your path. This can be either *internal* or *external motivation.*

Internal motivation is things you do to support your decision to make changes in your life, such as reinforcing positive behavior with rewards or posting inspirational messages in places where you will see them frequently.

Be creative. For example, if your goal is to lose weight, find a photo of yourself at your fattest, have it blown up and tape it to the door of your refrigerator. This will cause you to think twice when you sneak into the kitchen for a late night snack.

External motivation is when other people encourage and support you to success. These can be loved ones and friends, professionals like therapists and life coaches, and even experts who have written books or produced videos that inspire you.

The more internal and external motivation you use to keep you on your chosen path, the more enthusiastic you will become about your journey and the more likely you will be to succeed and achieve your Power Goals.

Interrupting Negative Behavior

Inevitably, there will be setbacks. Nobody is perfect and you will occasionally fail or succumb to temptation. It is possible, however, to short circuit this bad behavior by attempting to interrupt negative behavior as soon as you recognize the triggers associated with your bad habit.

While you were developing the self-awareness that led to the recognition of your bad habit, you identified a series of triggers or patterns that usually preceded your acting on your bad habit. These can be thoughts you have or physical sensations like sights or smells that tempt you.

Often, simply avoiding these types of triggers is enough to keep you on track. But if you accidentally or unknowingly trip one of these triggers, you can interrupt your potential negative behavior by removing yourself from that situation. Drop everything and go in the opposite direction. Stop the thought process that is going to lead you to trouble.

For example, if your bad habit is alcoholism and you unexpectedly run into an old "drinking buddy", think of an excuse to get away from that person as quickly as possible. The longer you spend with that person, the higher the chances that your desire to have a drink will be triggered.

Keeping Focused on the Benefits of Good Habits

Overcoming temptation can be difficult, especially at the beginning of your journey to break your bad habit. One effective way that can help you is to remind yourself of why you want to break the habit in the first place.

Earlier, you identified the benefits of replacing your bad habit with a good one. These benefits were boiled down into your personal Vision Statement. Keep this handy so that you can revisit it whenever you need to. Keep a copy of your Vision Statement in your wallet or purse so that you can pull it out and read it when you become tempted to recede back to your earlier bad behavior.

Often, simply reminding yourself of what you want out of life and how avoiding temptation in the moment will help you achieve your goal in the long term is enough to give you the strength to make better choices.

Reward and Punishment

Conditioning is a term used in psychology to describe the process of using reward and punishment to affect behavior. Experimental subjects can be taught learned behavior by being given rewards or by being punished when they fail to take a desired action.

Conditioning also is applicable to real life. You work at your job because you are rewarded with a paycheck. You pay your taxes because you want to avoid the punishment of going to jail for tax evasion.

When breaking a bad habit, using small rewards to reinforce positive behavior is an excellent way to keep you motivated and to associate happy, healthy emotions with the positive choices you make.

If, for example, your goal is to lose 30 lbs within six months, build in a reward structure that reinforces your hitting various milestones: Buying yourself a new outfit every time you lose five pounds or treat yourself to a spa treatment when you reach the halfway point.

Punishment, however, is less effective because invariably people will figure out a way to exploit a punishment structure in order to "authorize" unwanted behavior. Not much tends to get accomplished under this model.

For example, if your bad habit is swearing and you create a punishment structure in which you have to pay $1 into a piggy bank every time you use a curse word, you may find yourself saving up your money so that you can curse at will. In other words, the punishment becomes "worth it" in order to perform the bad behavior. This is not a positive way to proceed.

Punishment also sustains negative thoughts with your bad habit. When you punish yourself, it negatively affects your self-esteem: "I'm such a terrible person that I deserve to be punished". The idea is to build positivity and optimism, not reinforce poor self-image and pessimism.

So when it comes to breaking bad habits, use plenty of carrots but stay away from the stick!

Eliminating Negativity

You will be more likely to achieve your Power Goals if you eliminate as much negativity from your life as possible. This includes both *internal* and *external negativity*.

Internal negativity includes thoughts and feelings you have about yourself that are critical, damaging to your self-esteem, and pessimistic. Be aware of when these types of thoughts and emotions start to creep up and simply expel them from your mind. Through the power of will, you can decide to think positively and stop negative thinking.

External negativity can be more challenging to stop. These are things that other people say to you or express non-verbally that are critical or damaging to your self-esteem. They include such things as hurtful comments from your boss, nagging from your wife, or "teasing" from your friends. If you want to improve your chances of achieving your Power Goals it's necessary that you *shut them down* or *shut them out*.

Shutting them down means standing up to whoever is being critical of you and explaining to them that you aren't interested in their opinion or that what they are saying is hurtful and that you aren't going to listen to them anymore. This requires a little bit of backbone, but it is an effective way to shut down naysayers and boost your confidence at the same time.

Still, it's not always practical. For example, if you are receiving your annual review and your boss is being critical of your job performance, you probably aren't going to tell him off, at least not if you want to keep your job. In these types of instances, you can shut them out.

Just because somebody has a negative opinion of you or says something mean or nasty to you doesn't mean that you have to listen to them. Shut them out by not paying attention to what they are saying or letting it roll off you like water off a duck's back.

Negativity is the enemy of your journey to achieve your Vision Statement and, as a result, needs to be banished from your life in whatever form it takes.

THE GAME PLAN

You have developed self-awareness so that you recognize your bad habits, made a personal commitment to replace them with good habits, developed a Vision Statement to guide you to where you want to go, and created Power Goals that will take you there.

The next step is to create a Game Plan that will break your journey down into achievable steps. In my opinion, this is the most enjoyable part of breaking bad habits and replacing them with good ones because you get to build the structure you will use over the course of the next several days or months to turn your goals into reality.

Drawing Up Your Game Plan

Your Game Plan is an action plan, just like generals draw up when planning to lead their armies into combat or captains of industry use to plan an expansion or to increase profits.

It is going to be a real, tangible plan that includes measurements that can be observed, built-in rewards to motivate you to reach both short- and long- term objectives, and has a concluding achievement: Living your Vision Statement every day so that you can be happy and productive.

It begins with your Power Goals. Pull these out and consider how long it will realistically take for you to achieve each of them. Don't be overly indulgent. Your Game Plan should challenge you to reach your objectives as quickly as you can. The more time you allow yourself to persist with your bad habit, the harder it will be to break.

Let's look at an example of what a Game Plan might look like. Assume the bad habit you want to break is that you gamble too much and that you currently go to the casino every Friday and Saturday night, buy lottery tickets daily, go to the racetrack every Sunday and bet on sports several times per week. That's a lot of gambling!

When identifying your Power Goals, the "Family" goal you set was:

Family – My addiction to gambling means I spend little time with my spouse and children. I also spend a large percentage of my income on my gambling, to the extent that there is often not enough to buy groceries or pay my children's tuition.

Power Goal – Stop gambling so that I can be home more and be supportive of my family both emotionally and financially.

In this instance, quitting cold turkey may not have a high percentage of success. You may have tried to quit numerous times before, but always receded back into your bad habit.

Instead, your Power Goal can be broken down into a series of steps that are achievable and come with a built-in reward structure:

1. By the end of Week 1, I will cut up my membership card to the casino's VIP club, stop betting on sports, and only buy one lottery ticket per week. At the end of the week, with the money I save I will take my family out to dinner at a restaurant.

2. By the end of Week 2, I will end my Sunday "tradition" of going to the track and will limit my visits to the casino to one night per week. With the money I save, I will pay my children's past due tuition.

3. By the end of Week 3, I will voluntarily put myself on the casino's "banned patrons" list and not buy any lottery

tickets. This will end my gambling habit. As a reward, I will commit to planning at least one fun family activity each weekend, such as going to the zoo or going camping.

Notice that there is no punishment involved with failing. If you don't succeed in meeting your commitment for the week, restart the clock and try again until you succeed. As long as you stay committed and focused, eventually you will make your way through your entire Game Plan.

Asking for Help

Some bad habits are so powerful that it's nearly impossible to overcome them on your own. Addictions to drugs, alcohol, gambling, sex and other life-threatening habits may require you to get professional help, as well as the support and assistance of your family and friends.

It's natural not to want to ask for help. People's personal pride or even embarrassment often gets in the way. But if your bad habit is so strong that you aren't going to be able to break it without help, then you need to set your reluctance aside and turn to other people to help you.

Think of it this way: There is no shame in wanting to be a better person. Even though it may seem to you that other people may think less of you if you admit that you have a problem, in reality most people are going to give you credit for trying to do something about it.

Training Wheels: Easing into New Habits

With very few exceptions, going cold turkey or trying to break a bad habit immediately is not going to be effective. Because it has taken you so long to develop your bad habit, it's going to take at least a little time for you to break it.

You can improve your chances of success by easing into your new good habits, rather than going "all in" from the outset. Slowly wean yourself off of your bad habit (but not too slowly!) and introduce your new, good habit until eventually you are completely free of the bad and committed to the good.

For example, if your bad habit is that you drink too much, you may want to start by drinking less and replacing some of the time you spent drinking at bars taking long walks or even joining a gym. As the weeks progress, you can ease off the drinking altogether and replace your negative behavior with positive behavior. In time, it's possible you will become "addicted" to working out, eating right and living a healthier lifestyle.

Timelines and Milestones

In most case, it takes 21 days or a month to break a bad habit. It's helpful, although not essential, that you start your Game Plan on the first day of a new month. This simply makes it easier to set up the timelines and milestones you will need to ease yourself into your new positive behavior patterns. If you can't wait until the start of a new month then at least wait until the beginning of the new week, if possible.

When you are developing your Game Plan, don't just take it week at a time. In other words, don't just plan the first week's goals and see how it goes from there. To improve your chances of success, plan out the entire Game Plan over multiple weeks until you reach your ultimate Power Goal.

When creating your Game Plan, every new week should build on the success of the week before so that by the end of the process you have completely eliminated the bad habit you wanted to break and replaced with a good habit which will improve the quality of your life and push you toward achieving your Vision Statement.

Dealing with Setbacks

Know ahead of time that you are going to experience setbacks. The trick is not to let failure derail the entire process.

One of the benefits of having a Game Plan is that if you fail to reach a particular week's goals, you don't have to start over from the beginning. You can just restart that particular week and move everything up a week. All the other progress you already have made can be salvaged.

If you experience a setback, don't just gloss over it and bull through you Game Plan. It happened for a reason. Maybe you were moving too fast or didn't realize how much time you needed to achieve a particular step in your journey. Go back and repeat the step until you get it right. Only then should you move on to the next step.

Remaining Positive

It's critical that you not let your setbacks cause you to fall back into negative thinking. Mistakes are going to be made. We are all only human. Accept that you are fallible and move on. But don't dwell on the fact that you have failed or think of yourself as a failure.

The very fact that you are trying to make your life better means that you are the **opposite** of a failure. Even if you don't succeed all the time – and you won't -- you can still be successful. Even Joe DiMaggio failed to get a hit more than 60% of the time.

The most important thing is to stay positive and to just keep trying. As long as you are making the effort to get better, you are a winner.

STRATEGIES FOR SUCCESSFUL
HABIT FORMATION

Let's return for a moment to our definition of a habit. A habit – whether it is good or bad – is something we do without thinking about it. Habitual behavior happens automatically. It's part of who we are and how we live our lives.

In order to learn a new good habit, we have to literally teach ourselves to repeatedly do that habit until we do it reflexively, without thinking about it.

For example, if the bad habit we broke was driving too fast and the good habit we want to nurture is following the speed limit, we would have to force ourselves to drive the speed limit every time we got behind the wheel until we reached the point where we did it without thinking. Eventually, through repetition, it becomes second nature to us.

Using Reminders

Information overload is a very real condition in contemporary society, and it's only getting worse. Now that people can connect to the Internet from their smart phones and tablets and stream video anywhere and anytime they want, the result is shorter attention spans.

It's incredibly easy to become distracted now. There are just so much other stimuli to attract your attention. So staying on course with your Power

Goals and following your Game Plan is going to take a total and genuine commitment on your part.

One helpful way to remind yourself to stay on track is through the use of reminders. These can be little things such as Post-It notes, text messages, emails and voicemails you can either send to yourself or have somebody else send you so that you are bombarded with reminders that will keep you motivated and focused on your goal.

Reminders are especially helpful if they are used in conjunction with your trigger points. If there is a particular place or event that reminds you of your past bad habit, use creative ways to post reminders to yourself so that you can avoid the temptation of recidivism. For example, if your bad habit is that you drink too much and your trigger point is the family liquor cabinet, install a padlock on the cabinet and give the key to your spouse to hide.

The Power of Ritual

If you the same thing at the same time every day, it can become a *ritualized experience*. For example, you probably have a "morning ritual" which dictates when you shower, drink coffee, use the bathroom, get dressed and prepare for work. You probably follow the same exact sequence every day so that you don't even have to think about it.

This same type of ritualized experience can be applied to your newly developed good habits. Train yourself to perform the same actions at the same time and in the same sequence every day until they become second nature. That way you will gain the benefits of your good habits without having to consciously choose to do them.

All Together Now: Grouping Actions

Grouping actions is when you take a number of good habits and perform them all at the same time. This saves you time and, once you make them part of your routine, you will do them automatically.

For example, if the bad habit you want to break is poor personal hygiene, you could group together good habits like brushing your teeth, using mouthwash, showering, shaving, applying deodorant and putting on clean cloths so that they are always performed ritually at the same time every day.

In many cases, it is far easier to use group actions than to try to remember to do each of the good habits individually.

Keys to Consistency

Something is a habit if it doesn't require any thought on your part. Try to ensure your new good habit is performed consistently by repeating it every day for 21 or 30 days. When you keep doing the same thing over and over at the same time and place and in the same sequence, you will begin to consistently follow your new good habit as second nature.

This helps create a permanent good habit that is drilled into your daily routine, rather than having multiple habits that are loosely connected.

Utilizing Your Personal Rhythms

You already have set routines that you follow at work, at home and even when you socialize. Try linking new habits with existing ones rather than trying to install a completely new routine. This will make it easier to absorb the new positive habit into your life and will speed up how quickly it becomes part of your ritual.

For example, if your bad habit is that you are disorganized, one of your Power Goals might be to set some time aside every day to organize what you want to accomplish that day. An existing habit you have is that you always shower the moment you wake up. You can fit your new habit into your existing habit by using your shower time to map out your day. You could even go so far as to install a whiteboard in your shower stall where you can jot down your key objectives for the day. Be as creative as possible!

LIVING POSITIVELY

One of the things many people aren't prepared for is success. Ironically, some people have failed so many times before that when they finally achieve success in breaking a bad habit, they have trouble coping with it, which can send them spiraling back down to where they began.

This is because they usually have some sort of mental block that prevents them from accepting the fact that they are powerful and willful and that once they set their mind to something, they have the ability to see it through to the very end. Removing these types of mental blocks and using the power of your mind to achieve and sustain your success is essential to reaching your long term objectives as defined by your Vision Statement.

Thoughts, Belief Structures and Habits

Sometimes your mind can put limits on what you can accomplish. For example, if your bad habit is that you overeat and your Power Goal is to lose 15 lbs. in 30 days, if your mind has a defeatist or pessimistic outlook it's going to be more difficult for you to reach your goal. In other words, the mind often leads the body.

So it's important that you train your mind to reject negativity and embrace positivity. It's possible to reprogram your mind so that success comes more easily. All you need to do is to have beliefs that are supportive of your goal and your reality will line up with your beliefs.

Remember, habits operate on the subconscious level and are based on the things we believe or once believed. So even if you purge a negative belief from your mind ("I'm too fat" or "I have no self-control"), if you allow negativism to be sustained and don't quash it, that negative thought will only be replaced with another one ("I'm not strong enough to do this").

Affirmations and Declarations

Dispelling negativity from our worldview is easier said than done. For almost your entire life, your negative thoughts have been reinforced by your bad habits. In your mind, you believe you will fail to achieve your Power Goal because you have always failed in the past, right?

Not necessarily! There is a technique you can use to banish negativity from your mind and replace it with positive thoughts. It's called using *affirmations* and *declarations*.

Affirmations are short phrase you repeat to yourself several times a day, usually while looking at yourself in a mirror. They are designed to reprogram your mind to reinforce positive and banish negativity. They can include such phrases as:

"I am a powerful, willful person."

"I can accomplish anything I set my mind to."

"I am strong enough to do whatever I truly want." "I am a happy person who deserves success."

Affirmations can also be habit-centric:

"I am going to be sober today."

"I will spend my day smoke-free."

"I am going to stay out of the casino today."

By their definition, affirmations are positive statements. So avoid affirmations that use the words "won't" or "not".

Affirmations are a helpful way to focus the mind on the positive and they really work. Develop three or four affirmations that are relevant to your Power Goals and repeat them to yourself out loud in front of mirror ten times each three times a day for a week. At the end of that time, you will notice a change in the way you feel about yourself. You will have more positive energy and negative thoughts will have been banished from your worldview, at least when it comes to our bad habit.

Declarations are statements that you make to other people about yourself. Like affirmations, they work by defining who you are, in both your own mind and to others.

For example, people who attend Alcoholics Anonymous meetings always start out their "sharing" by saying, "My name is (whatever your name is) and I'm an alcoholic." The other people at the meeting show their support and acceptance by greeting them by name. With their declaration, the person both accepts responsibility by publicly declaring that they have a problem and is simultaneously supported by the group.

Affirmations and declarations are an effective way to build positivity and expel negative thinking from your mind. You may feel a little silly using them at first, but once you start to realize the benefits, that embarrassment will soon be replaced by feelings of empowerment.

Visualization and Positivity

Another technique to promote positivity is to use *visualization exercises*. This is when you set aside a little time every day to visualize what your life is going to look like once you replace our bad habits with good ones.

Try it out for yourself by finding a quiet place where you won't be interrupted for at least five to ten minutes. Sit comfortably and close your eyes. Try to relax completely. When your mind is calm, don't dwell on your bad habit or its consequences, but instead imagine what your daily life will look like once you adopt your new good habit.

Be as detailed as you possibly can. What will you look like? What will other people say to you? What will you smell? What do you feel? What thoughts are you having?

Visualization helps prepare the mind for success by anticipating that success. Then, when you begin to realize the positive consequences of your good habits, you are less likely to reject them with negativity. There are even some people who believe that it is possible to actively influence events by visualizing them. In other words, simply believing that positive things are going to happen to you can actually cause positive things to happen.

While there may or may not be any direct correlation between the two, it's absolutely true that preparing your mind for success through visualization makes it easier for you to embrace that success once it arrives.

Making a Vision Board

Different people learn in different ways. Some people are doers and need to get their hands dirty by actually performing a specific task in order for their minds to absorb it. Others can simply read a book or watch a video and be able to learn how to do something.

Other people, however, are visual learners who need to physically see something repeatedly before it is absorbed into their minds. For these, there are *vision boards*

Vision boards are collections of photographs, images, quotes, videos and anything else that positive reinforces what you are trying to accomplish. It can be a collage made of cardboard and magazine clippings or a digital web page you build on Pinterest or another website.

In either case, the purpose of the vision board is to provide positive visual reinforcement for your objective. By frequently looking at your vision board, you mentally train your mind to think positively about your journey. This can ease the process of making positive decisions and avoiding negativity.

The Power of Hypnosis

While hypnosis may have a bad reputation among some people thanks to carnival frauds and phony party entertainers, hypnotism is an actual physiological process that is widely used in psychology and psychiatry to treat a variety of mental conditions.

When performed by a trained professional, hypnosis puts the subject in a deeply relaxed trance-like state then places post-hypnotic suggestions into the person's subconscious. These suggestions then become embedded into their belief system, but only if they are already disposed to the suggestion in the first place. You couldn't hypnotize somebody to believe in God if they are already an agnostic or atheist, or to vote Democratic if they are a Republican, for example.

So somebody who is struggling to quit smoking can be hypnotized to believe that whenever they smoke a cigarette it tastes like poison. When the person comes out of the hypnotic state, that suggestion remains part or their belief system so whenever they smoke, the bad taste is so anxiety- causing that they are unable to finish the cigarette.

If you are interested in using hypnosis to help you break your bad habit, ask your doctor or health care professional to refer you to a reputable professional hypnotist.

There also are less costly shortcuts you can find online that use self- hypnosis programs created by professionals. The self- hypnosis tapes and CDs you buy online help you relax so you can address your root problems and break bad habits.

Meditation and Clarity

You have already used a form of meditation when you performed your visualization exercise. Meditation works the same way: You find a quiet place where you won't be disturbed and you put yourself into a relaxed state. The difference is that with meditation, instead of visualizing yourself as being successful, you clear your mind completely of all thought.

When you are in a meditative state, your mind is a blank page. There are no distractions or anxieties to occupy your mind: In fact, there is nothing at all. For a period of time – usually anywhere from 10 to 30 minutes – you empty your mind of everything.

When you come out of a meditative state, you will feel relaxed and completely reinvigorated. Just 15 to 20 minutes of meditation can provide as much energy as a full night's sleep. Anxieties will be relieved and negative thoughts will be purged. Plus, your mind will have a sharpness and clarity that will help you think more clearly, empowering you to achieve your Power Goals more easily.

TAKING ACTION

The Chinese philosopher Confucius famously said, "The journey of a thousand miles begins with a single step." Even though he said those words more than 2,500 years ago, they are still as true today as the day they were spoken.

Now that you have a Game Plan that comes complete with a timetable, milestones, measurable objectives and rewards, the next step is to implement it. Making big changes in your life can be intimidating and can cause a lot of apprehension in many people, but by this point you should be confident in the idea that you truly want to make a genuine change in the direction your life is leading.

Focus and Willpower

The time and energy you spent creating your Game Plan will now pay off as you begin your journey. You know ahead of time where you need to be every step of the way and this will help to keep you focused and motivated.

Still, there are always going to be unpredictable eventualities and life is occasionally going to throw a curveball at you high and inside. Don't flinch. Stand your ground. The radical changes you are making now will have positive influences on every aspect of your life from here on out.

If you start to waver, use the techniques outlined in the last chapter – such as affirmations, a vision board, meditation and the rest – to keep on track.

Implementation

When you wake up on Day 1 of your program to break your bad habit and replace it with a good one, you may feel nervous or afraid. Take comfort in the fact that you have planned out every step of the way. You already have all the tools you need to overcome your bad habit, plus you have retrained your mind to be positive and to reject negativity.

Although the road is long, the steps are short. You can do this! Not only is success inevitable, given your motivation and the structure you have built to prepare for your journey, you are completely ready for this. You are strong, brave and capable.

Everything up to this point has been preface. Now is the moment when real, genuine and positive change begins. Are you excited? You should be!

Defeating Inertia

Newton's First Law of Physics states that an object in motion tends to stay in motion and that objects at rest tend to stay at rest. This law can easily be applied to habits. It's far easier to stay the way you are rather than change. But without change, there can be no growth. And without growth, you are not going to achieve the success that you desire.

Fortunately, you don't need to apply an overwhelming force in order to get the ball rolling. The tiniest of shoves in the right direction will start you on your path. As you progress through your Game Plan, achieving your objectives along the way, you can gain momentum so that before you know it you have passed the halfway point to your goal, then the three-quarters point and, finally, you will have the finish line in sight!

The Dangers of "All or Nothing"

Something is better than nothing. Even the smallest of accomplishments is favorable to continued failure. While your ultimate objective may be something quite challenging, it usually isn't realistic to expect you to jump from Point A to the finish line in one single step. It simply doesn't work that way.

Avoid taking an "all or nothing" approach to breaking your bad habit. It will lead to nothing but frustration. In most cases, a bad habit can be overcome using smaller, more achievable steps that are supported by positivity and continual motivation, both internal and external.

Accepting Incremental Improvements

It's okay if you don't eat the whole enchilada in one bite. Indeed, it's preferable to take small bites rather than choking to death or overburdening your digestive tract.

In the same way, it's okay to take it slowly when breaking a bad habit. Your bad habit didn't develop overnight and you shouldn't expect to overcome it instantly.

For example, if your bad habit is that you use heroin, going cold turkey is going to be a tortured, agonizing experience. In fact, it could shock your system to the point where the cure is worse than the disease. Depending on your level of addiction, it may even kill you. More often than not, it's not going to work anyway.

A better plan would be to wean yourself off the drug slowly under the care of a trusted medical professional. They will normally recommend that you substitute a less powerful narcotic, such as methadone, so that the process of eliminating your addiction is more achievable.

Even if your bad habit isn't as radical as that, the same principles apply. Be accepting of incremental improvements. Ultimately, they will lead to total victory over your bad habit.

Embracing Failure

For somebody with a negative perspective, failure is something terrible, scary and should be avoided at all costs. But for the positive-thinking person, failure is an opportunity.

As human beings, we learn through failure. It's the "error" part of trial and error that leads to the greatest discoveries. When you have a setback on your journey or you fail to achieve your Game Plan's weekly objective, use it as a learning tool to identify what went wrong and why so that you can avoid making the same mistake again.

The beauty of the Breaking the Habit program is that if you fail it's not necessary that you go all the way back to the beginning. You can simply repeat the step you slipped up on again so that you can keep your forward momentum going.

Power of Persistence

The movie "Rocky" is one of my favorite films of all time. As you may recall, the titular character, Rocky Balboa, played by a very young Sylvester Stallone, is a working class Philadelphia boxer who through extraordinary circumstances gets the opportunity of a lifetime to fight the heavyweight champion of the world, Apollo Creed.

Everybody remembers the mesmerizing and inspirational moment at the end of that movie, when the music swells and Rocky is showered with adulation as he is reunited with his shy, awkward girlfriend, Adrian.

But what many people don't remember is that Rocky didn't win his fight against Apollo Creed. He lost the match on a decision. But that didn't stop Rocky from becoming one of the most beloved movie characters of all time because he accomplished his intended goal: He "went the distance" against the best boxer in the world. By getting up and coming back for more whenever he got knocked down, Rocky became a winner.

Like Rocky, you can be the hero of your own movie as long as you keep getting up and coming back for more. The glory isn't in the destination, it's in the journey. By using the power of your own persistence, you will overcome your bad habit and change it into a good one, regardless of the blows you receive along the way.

You may not win every battle and sometimes, like Rocky, you are even going to get your ass kicked. But as long as you keep fighting, you will be the champion.

KEEPING SCORE

In order to assure that you get the outcome you want and stay motivated and on track, it's critical that you record your progress and review and refine your Game Plan as you progress through your program.

You mapped out your Game Plan from a safe distance before you got into the heat of the action. There probably were things that you didn't anticipate happening. It's okay to make changes. Your Game Plan is a guideline, not a rule book. As long as it gets you to where you want to go within the timeframe that you have planned for yourself, it can be adapted and modified as much or as little as you like.

Just make sure that your program is progressing towards your goal, not backsliding back into the bad habit you are trying to break.

A Record of Your Success

Keep a record of your performance versus your Game Plan. I like to call this the "Victory Log". This will help you measure and see your progress as you move through your program. It also will help you put together your next Game Plan when you are ready to break another bad habit.

In your Victory Log, record your performance versus your objective. Identify shortcomings. Be honest and unflinching. The Victory Log is for your eyes only.

Ultimately, when you reach your objective, your Habit Diary and your Victory Log can help point to the key elements that led to your success. These key elements can then be applied to other areas of your life so that you can make constant, positive improvements and move closer to realizing your Vision Statement.

Weekly Progress Reviews

Schedule a time to review your success each week. Make it a new good habit by making it at the same time and day every week, making it easier to remember to do it. Eventually, you will start to look forward to this time because the closer you get to your objective, the more likely it will be that the news will be good.

Weekly progress reviews should be as non-judgmental as possible. Update your Victory Log without emotion, explaining exactly what you did well and what you didn't. Any setback of failure should be accompanied by a plan of action to correct those areas where you need improvement. These can then be folded into the Game Plan for subsequent weeks.

Celebrating Victories

The little rewards you built into your Game Plan are important motivators, so don't skip them. Even if they are simply trinkets or tokens, because you had to earn them they will take on deeply personal significance.

For example, people who are struggling with alcoholism and who embark on the 12-Step program are presented with chips that celebrate various stages of their sobriety. These cheap plastic chips are presented for 30- days, six-months, one-year and 10-years of sobriety. While these chips may not have any actual monetary value, for the people who earn them they are among their most valuable possessions.

When your Game Plan has been completed and you have achieved your overall objective, it's time to celebrate. Invite loved ones to join you at a celebratory dinner or throw a party. Not only do you deserve it, but celebrating your achievement will reinforce your positive behavior and make it easier to repeat the process when it's time to address other bad habits you want to correct.

Taking It to the Next Level

You've made it through your first Game Plan. You've broken a bad habit and replaced it with a good one. Now what?

You still have your Vision Statement to achieve. Build on the experience and success of your first Game Plan and apply those lessons to the next bad habit you want to correct.

Where does it stop? You know you have reached your ultimate goal when your Vision Statement is no longer a target you want to achieve, but actually describes your everyday life.

Breaking the Habit Permanently

This may be the end of this guide, but it's not the end of the road for you. There are still many bad habits to correct before you are living the life you have always imagined for yourself. But now that you are armed with the knowledge of how to achieve this, the experience of breaking your first bad habit will give you the confidence you need to continue your journey.

I said at the very beginning that you have the power to do whatever you set your mind to do. Now you know the truth in that statement. Keep believing in yourself and never, ever, ever give up.

You can change your world. You just have to do it one habit at a time! Good luck!

Printed by Libri Plureos GmbH in Hamburg, Germany